T0365501

Playing With Rain

Sandi White

Copyright © 2010, 2021 by Sandi White. 50160-WHIT

All rights reserved. No part of this book may
be reproduced or transmitted in any form or by
any means, electronic or mechanical, including
photocopying, recording, or by any information storage
and retrieval system, without permission in writing from
the copyright owner.

This is a work of fiction. Names, characters,
places and incidents either are the product of the
author's imagination or are used fictitiously, and any
resemblance to any actual persons, living or dead,
events, or locales is entirely coincidental.

To order additional copies of this book, contact:
Xlibris
844-714-8691
www.Xlibris.com
Orders@Xlibris.com

ISBN: Softcover   978-1-4500-1534-9
         Hardcover   978-1-4500-1535-6
         EBook   978-1-4771-7771-6

Library of Congress Control Number: 2009913828

Print information available on the last page

Rev. date: 01/13/2021

Dedicated to:

Playing with Rain is dedicated to my daughter, Nyda Thompkins. It was written for her when she was eight years old, she's now nineteen. The book is also dedicated to to Nyda's god-sister, Tishara Samuel, daughter of my best friend, Heidi Lewis. Tishara has always supported my efforts to self publish my book.

Long, long time ago, Rain never wet children. It only wet parents. Rain used to follow children home from school or church. It would stop to let them play in the sun as long as they wanted to, then follow them again.

长，长时间前，雨不湿儿童。 它只湿父母。 用来按照儿童家庭学校或教堂的雨。它会停止让他们只要他们想在太阳中播放，然后再跟进。

Largo, hace mucho tiempo, los niños nunca húmedos de lluvia. Sólo había húmedo los padres. Lluvia utiliza para seguir niños casas de la escuela o iglesia. Podría detener a desempeñar en el sol, rnientras: que querían, a continuaci6n, seguirlas de nuevo.

Then one day, when the children came out of school, Sun was nowhere to be found. There was light, but no Sun. He was sick and was resting behind a cloud. So the children went home, hoping to see him the next day. Rain followed behind, leaving puddles everywhere, but being careful not to wet the children.

一天的学校，儿童何时太阳当时无处找。 此外，我们没有轻，但没有太阳。
他是病，休息背后一群。 因此儿童回家，希望看到他翌日。
雨后背后，地方，离开陪衬但切勿湿儿童。

A continuación, un dia, cuando los niños llegó fuera de la escuela, Sun fue ninguna parte se encuentra. Allí se fue luz, pero no Sun. Fue enfermo y se descansar detrás de una nube. Asi que los niños fueron a casa, esperando Veele al dia siguiente. Lluvia seguido detrás dejando puddles en todas partes, pero teniendo cuidado de no mojarse 10s niñios.

6

The next day, still no Sun. He was still sick. The children were sad. They wanted to play in the sun. They started home from school with Rain following close behind, but not wetting them.

"Maybe I can play with the children," thought Rain.

But she didn't know how. This made her sad.

下一个的天仍没有太阳。 他是仍病。 儿童是悲哀。 他们想在太阳中播放。他们开始主页学校有雨后关闭后，但不是湿他们。

"也许我可以玩孩子，"认为雨。

但她 didn't 知道如何。 这使她悲哀。

El día siguiente, no todavía Sun. Fue aún enfermo. Los niños eran tristes. Querían que desempeñar en el sol. Comenzaron inicio de la escuela con lluvia tras cerrar detrás, pero no enuresis les.

The third day came and still no Sun. The children were sadder. They slowly walked home from school with Rain carefully following them. She was sadder too. She wanted to help the children, but didn't know what to do.

第三天并仍没有太阳。 儿童是人。 他们慢慢走主页从学校有雨仔细后他们。 她也人。 她想帮助儿童，但 didn't 知道怎样做。

El tercer día vino y no todavía Sun. Los niños eran más triste. Lentamente anduvieron inicio de la escuela con lluvia cuidadosamente tras les. También fue más triste. Ella queria ayudar a los niños y :niñas, pero didn't sabe que hacer.

After school on the fourth day, Sun was still sick and could not come out to play.

Rain said, "I will play with you."

"How?" asked the children.

"Can you play hopscotch?" asked one little girl.

"Sure," said Rain. "I've seen you play it with Sun before."

第四个当日课余太阳仍病并不能播放出来。

雨说："我会担当与您"。

"如何？"要求儿童。

"可以播放跳飛機吗?"要求一个小女孩。

"确保"说雨。"我 've 看到您玩前的太阳"

Después de la escuela en el cuarto día, el sol fue aún enfermo y no puede venire a jugar.

Lluvia dijo, "se juego con usted."

"Cómo?" pidió una niña pequeña.

"Seguro," dijo lluvia. "yo visto reproducirlo con Sun antes."

So another little girl drew the boxes in the dirt and took her turn. Everyone else had their turn. Now it was Rain's turn. But the boxes all turned to mud and puddles.

因此另一个小女孩制订框中，污垢并她打开。所有其他人有其打开。现在是雨's 打开。但所有框泥，陪衬。

Tan otra niña dibujó las casillas en la tierra y tomó su turno. Todos los demás tuvo a su vez. Ahora es gire la's lluvia. Pero los cuadros de todos se didica a barro y los puddles

Then one boy suggested to draw the boxes on the sidewalk with chalk. But when it was Rain's turn again, the chalk all washed away.

然后一名男童建议与粉笔人行道上绘制框。 但当它是雨's再次，打开冲走所有粉笔。

A continuación, un niño sugirió para dibujar de las casillasen la vereda con tiza. Pero cuando se activar que's lluvia de nuevo, la tiza todos destruida.

Everyone said, "It's no use."

"Everything will get wet and washed away," said another boy.

So the children started home with Rain sadly following them.

大家都说" 它 's 没有用 "。

" 一切将获取湿和冲走 ， " 说另一名男童。

因此儿童主页开始有雨遗憾的是以下他们。

Todos lo dicho, "es's no"

" Todo se obtener húmedo y destruida," dijo otro muchacho

Así que los niños comenzó, inicio, con lluvia Lamentablemente tras les.

Suddenly, the children stopped to chat a little. Rain, who was so sad, was not looking at the children and passed right over them.

突然，儿童有点停止聊天。 雨曾如此悲哀，不看儿童，权利通过他们。

De repente, los niños detenido para charlar un poco. Lluvia, que era tan triste, no estaba mirando de los niños y pasado derecho sobre ellos

Everyone began to scream.

Rain stopped and cried, "I'm sorry, so sorry."

She stopped wetting the children.

每个人都开始遗憾。

雨停止和哭 " 我 'm 对不起，所以对不起 "。

她停止湿儿童。

Todo el mundo de comenzó a gritar.

Lluvia detenido y clamó, " 'm lo siento, asi que lo siento."

Ella detuvo enuresis los niños.

The children just stood around, sadly looking at each other. All of them wet from head to toe.

儿童只站约，遗憾的看彼此。 所有这些湿从头，脚趾。

Los niños solo se alrededor, lamentablemente mirando mutuamente. Todos ellos húmedo de la cabeza a los pies.

Then a small boy jumped into a puddle and stomped. Then he jumped into another puddle and jumped up and down laughing. The other children looked at him, then at each other.

小男孩跳到一个　puddle　然后　stomped。　然后他跳到另一个　puddle，并跳上下笑。其它儿童看他，然后在每个其他。

Luego, un niño pequeño saltó en un charco y stomped. A continuación, él, saltó en otro Charco y saltó arriba y abajo riendo. Los otros niños studio él, a continuación, a cada uno de los otros.

Then everyone started laughing. They all ran and jumped into puddles. They stomped and jumped and laughed and giggled and made fun of how each other looked wet.

然后每个人都开始笑。 他们所有运行和跳到陪衬。 他们 stomped 跳和笑和 giggled 和作出的如何互相研究湿的乐趣。

A continuación, todos inició riendo. Todos corrió y saltó en puddles. Stomped y saltó reí y giggled y había hecho diversion de cómo mutuamente miró húmedo.

When Rain saw this, she was very happy. She was laughing so hard that a big shower covered the children. And that made them laugh and play even more.

当雨看到这时，她很高兴。 她笑因此硬大淋浴包括儿童。 ，作出笑，发挥更多。

Cuando lluvia vio esto, estab muy feliz. Ella se rien tan dificil que una gran ducha cubierto los niños. Y que les reir u jugar aum mas

They continued this way all the way home. When their parents saw them playing in the rain, they ran out with umbrellas and raincoats to get them.

他们继续这方式所有方式家庭。 当父母看到他们播放雨中，他们运行出伞与他们的 raincoats。

Esto siguieron el modo todo el camino a casa. Cuando sus padres vieron jugando en la lluvia, ejecuto fuero con paraguas y raincoats para obtenerles.

But the children knew if Sun did not come out to play the next day, they will have lots of fun playing with Rain. And to this day, that's what happens.

The End

但孩子知道是否太阳并不出来播放翌日，便大量逗弄雨的乐趣。 至今，'s 什么。

最后

Pero los niños sabian si Sun no proviene fuera que desempeñar al dia siguiente, se tienen mucha diversion jugando con lluvia. Y hasta el dia de hoy, "s lo que ocurre.

El Fin

Printed in the United States
By Bookmasters